SEIZE THE DAY
STUDY GUIDE

SEIZE THE DAY
STUDY GUIDE

Living on Purpose and Making
Every Day Count

JOYCE MEYER

NEW YORK · BOSTON · NASHVILLE

FaithWords
Hachette Book Group
1290 Avenue of the Americas, New York, NY 10104
faithwords.com
twitter.com/faithwords

First Edition: September 2016

FaithWords is a division of Hachette Book Group, Inc.
The FaithWords name and logo are trademarks of Hachette Book Group, Inc.

The publisher is not responsible for websites (or their content)
that are not owned by the publisher.

The Hachette Speakers Bureau provides a wide range of authors for speaking events. To find
out more, go to www.hachettespeakersbureau.com or call (866) 376-6591.

ISBN: 978-1-4555-4103-4

Printed in the United States of America

RRD-C

10 9 8 7 6 5 4 3 2 1

CONTENTS

This companion study guide is written to complete while reading *Seize the Day*. You may want to read the entire book and then come back and complete each chapter in this workbook, or you may want to go chapter by chapter in both books.

Whichever method you choose, I hope you will be honest and open with yourself, knowing that you do not need to share your answers. Being as open and honest as you can will help you identify areas in your life you need to surrender to God and ask for specific help.

I wrote this book to help you make the most of your days left on earth—to help you live on purpose.

I am usually a very goal-oriented individual, and I am motivated by accomplishment, so I stay on track. But in the past year I found myself looking at the piles of things I needed and wanted to do and became so double-minded about which one to do first that I often ended up doing nothing, or at best I just did little bits and pieces of several things—none of which I finished. Oh, I finished the things I absolutely had to do, but to be honest, I was wasting a lot of precious time and feeling aggravated at myself because I seemed to spend more time trying to figure out what to do than I did doing anything. I felt really overwhelmed.

That is unusual for me, so I really started praying about it and wanted to hear what God would say to me about the situation. I felt that life was ordering me around rather than me ordering my life, and I knew something was wrong.

As I prayed about it, God began showing me the importance of living life on purpose—something I had done most of my life but had somehow gotten away from.

I think part of the reason why I encountered the season of passivity and double-mindedness was so that I would feel an urgency to write this book. As I researched, I found that a large percentage of people live their lives day in and day out without accomplishing much of what they truly intend to. They are busy, but not sure what they are busy with.

"I'm busy" has become the standard excuse for all the things we should have done but didn't do. If you see a friend whom you used to hear from regularly, but now you cannot get them to return your calls, they will assuredly say, "I'm sorry I haven't called you back; I have just been very busy."

We recently waited almost three weeks to secure an appointment for a carpet bid. When we called the salesman for the third time, he said, "I'm sorry it has taken me so long to get back to you, we have just been so busy!" What if God never answered our calls and then gave the excuse of being too busy?

I truly wonder how many people at the end of their life feel they lived the life they were meant to live? How many have only regrets about the things they did or did not do during their life? You only have one life, and if it is not going in the direction that you want it to, now is the time to make changes.

If we live unproductive lives, we should not blame it on circumstances, other people, the way the world is today, or anything else. God created man and gave him free will. That means we have the ability to make choices in literally every area of life, and if we don't make our own choices guided by God, we will end up with nothing but regrets.

God has a will and purpose for each of us, and His desire is that we use our free will to choose His will so that we can enjoy the best life possible. I hope and pray that as you read this book you will learn to seize the day and start making the moments that you have count toward fulfilling your potential!

This study guide includes several parts to help you stay on track and digest all of the material in *Seize the Day*:

Get Ready prepares you for the subject matter in the chapter and reviews what was learned in the previous chapter.

Get Set digs into the heart of the chapter and gives you questions and activities to help you think more deeply about the subjects presented.

Go! is designed to help you implement the new ideas and strategies learned in the chapter.

Remember captures the main points of the chapter as well as a scripture to remember.

I hope you will use this book as a tool to choose to seize the day and live on purpose to honor God.

SEIZE THE DAY
STUDY GUIDE

CHAPTER 1

Man's Free Will

Get Ready...

Read Deuteronomy 30:19 in several Bible translations.

Then ask yourself which choice you are committed to making: Life or death? Blessings or curses?

_____

What do you need to do to choose life?

_____

_____

Get Set...

What does it mean to you to have free will? Journal about your thoughts on free will.

_____

_____

_____

_____

Are you more inclined to live in the summerhouse of your emotions, or the central citadel of your will? Explain.

_____

_____

_____

Reaping what we sow is a spiritual law that God has put into place in the universe, and it works the same way every time. If we sow to the flesh, we reap from the flesh ruin, decay, and destruction. But if we sow to the Spirit, we reap life (see Galatians 6:8). No matter how much bad seed (self-will and disobedience) anyone has planted, the moment they begin to plant good seed (obedience to God), their lives will begin to change for the better. God's mercy is new every morning—that means He has provided a way for us to begin fresh each day!

Do you truly believe that when we plant good seed—live in obedience to God—our lives change for the better? Explain.

_____

_____

_____

What do you need help with today to make better decisions?

_____

_____

_____

Write a prayer asking God for specific help. Take a few moments to be still and jot down any thoughts that come to mind that may help you make better choices.

_____

_____

_____

_____

Unless we learn the value of free will and begin to exercise it to make right choices, we will always be merely victims of life's circumstances and the bad choices those around us make. When I was a child and unable to make my own choices because I was under the authority of my parents, I was a victim of my mother and father's poor choices. But once I was away from home and had the ability to make my own choices, I was in a position to change my life. Sadly, I didn't know that, so I spent another eighteen years making wrong choices by acting according to my deceived mind and wounded emotions. At the age of thirty-six, through crying out for God's help, I received grace from Him to begin studying His Word. When I did, I discovered I could make choices according to God's will and, thus, become a victor instead of a victim.

Do you see yourself as a victor or a victim? Circle the term you identify with most and write why.

VICTIM   VICTOR

_____

_____

_____

Read the following scriptures and write how they can remind you to live as a victor and not a victim.

Romans 8:31–39

_____

_____

_____

II Timothy 1:6–10

_____

_____

_____

Philippians 4:11–13

_____

_____

_____

I Corinthians 15:54–57

_____

_____

_____

Go!

A great deal of the time God leads us by peace, wisdom, and common sense.
Think of a time in your life when you were led by each one. Write about it
to help you discern when God is leading you in the future.

Peace

_____

_____

_____

Wisdom

_____

_____

_____

Common sense

_____

_____

_____

Review David's story in II Samuel 11, 12:1–25. What sin did David commit against God?

_____

_____

_____

Read how David repented (read Psalm 51). Describe his words and actions.

_____

_____

_____

Use David as an example of how to change a wrong choice and follow God's will. Trust that God will forgive you, just as He forgave David, and commit to walking in God's will.

We don't have to manifest perfection in order to be accepted by God, but we do need to have a heart that is committed to always finding its way back to God's will.

Remember

We cannot always choose what our circumstances will be, but we can choose how we will respond to them. When we use our freedom to choose to do the will of God, He is honored and glorified.

Today I have given you the choice between life and death, between blessings and curses. Now I call on heaven and earth to witness the choice you make. Oh, that you would choose life, so that you and your descendants might live!

Deuteronomy 30:19 (NLT)

God's Will for Your Life

Before you begin, read chapter 2 in *Seize the Day*.

Get Ready...

Have you been more intentional in relying on God to help you make choices as you seek to follow His will? Share what you've done since completing chapter 1.

_____

_____

_____

Read the opening scripture, Psalm 40:8, in several translations. Ask yourself: Do you really delight in doing God's will? Why or why not?

_____

_____

_____

Get Set...

Wanting to know God's will is not primarily about our circumstances, our job, or whom we should marry. God does care about those things, but if we seek to know those answers alone, we are not discovering the most important part of God's will.

There are deeper things that God wants us to seek Him about, and when we do we will find that the answers we need for daily life are readily evident.

Read Matthew 6:33. How do you seek God's Kingdom and righteousness first?

_____

_____

Do a self-evaluation based on my list of deeper things God desires we seek Him about on pages 14–18.

Ask yourself:

1. Do I desire to know God more deeply and intimately? What am I doing to develop a closer relationship with God through Christ?

    _____

    _____

2. Am I striving each day to be more like Jesus with the help of the Holy Spirit? How?

    _____

    _____

3. Am I committed to diligent study of God's Word? How?

    _____

    _____

4. How much time do I spend learning about, reflecting on, and praying about love versus asking God for what I think I need or want?

    _____

    _____

5. Do I combat doubt, worry, or fear with faith? Explain.

   _____

   _____

6. Do I forgive myself and others when wronged? How free is my heart
   from offense?

   _____

   _____

7. How often do I thank God versus asking for things?

   _____

   _____

8. Am I gladly serving God?

   _____

   _____

*If you have been seeking God for His will concerning your life, I am ask-
ing that you first consider whether you are pursuing and growing in the
eight areas I mentioned. If you are not, set aside your other questions and go
after what God has already said is important to Him.*

Go!

Knowing God's will and actually doing it are two separate things. Think about
the things that hinder you from doing God's will all of the time. Jot them down.

_____

_____

How do you relate to Paul's assertion in Romans 7:19?

_____

_____

Do you understand the answer to the dilemma, as Paul did in Romans 7:25? Explain.

_____

_____

God wants us to use our free will to choose His will and then rely on Him and His grace to enable us to do it!

I think there are two mistakes we can make concerning the doing of God's will. First, we may try to do God's will using willpower alone, but then we experience frustration and disappointment because we always fail. Willpower is helpful, but it only takes us so far, and then we need supernatural power to step in.

Second, it is folly to think that we can have God's will without making a choice to do so. Passive people sit idly by and hope something good will happen to them, but they do nothing to ensure that it does. They may be deceived into thinking that if a thing is God's will, then God will just make it happen without them doing anything at all. For example, it is God's will for you to have a job if you need one, but you have to go look for one. We are partners with God. We have a part and He has a part. We cannot do His part, and He will not do our part.

Read the following scriptures and write how they describe our role in choosing and doing God's will.

John 15:5–8

_____

_____

_____

_____

James 1:22–25

_____

_____

_____

_____

I Corinthians 15:10

_____

_____

_____

We are in error if we think we can do what needs to be done on our own, and we are in error if we believe God will do everything for us. The Bible teaches us that God usually works in and through people to accomplish His will.

Review your prayer list from the past week. What have you prayed for most frequently?

_____

_____

_____

_____

Do your prayers show you are putting your desires first, or what God desires first?

_____

How can you change your focus to be more on what God desires?

_____

_____

_____

Read Jesus' prayer in John 17:1–26.

List who He prays for and what He prays for them.

_____

_____

_____

Read Jesus' prayer in Luke 22:42. How did His prayer show He was willing to do God's will?

_____

_____

How are your prayers similar to Jesus' prayer? Different?

_____

_____

_____

Making every day count is dependent on having a rich and vibrant relationship with God. Our prayers are important, and they don't have to be selfish and self-centered. Let's pray and then plan for God's will to be done each and every day in our lives.

How will you change your prayers today? Begin now by writing a prayer focusing more on God's will than yours. Use the eight areas of importance mentioned earlier to guide your prayer.

_____

_____

_____

Remember

By leaning entirely on Jesus—rather than on our own willpower—we can do what God wants us to do with His power (grace).

Pray like this:

Our Father in heaven, may your name be kept holy.

May your Kingdom come soon.

May your will be done on earth, as it is in heaven.

Matthew 6:9–10 (NLT)

Living for Eternity

Before you begin, read chapter 3 in *Seize the Day*.

Get Ready...

How has your prayer life changed since completing chapter 2? Have you done your part to develop a more intimate relationship with Christ? What have you experienced through this change?

_____

_____

_____

Read the opening scripture, the popular John 3:16, from several different translations.

   What does it mean to believe?

_____

_____

Have you chosen eternal life? How does your life reflect that choice?

_____

_____

Get Set...

Every moment we use is one that we never get back again, so using it wisely is important. Many people put off being in right relationship with God until another time. Usually it is because they want to do things they know God wouldn't approve of, so they think they will choose their own time. But what if they run out of time? It is a sobering question that can provoke us to more intercession for the lost.

How many truly live for eternity rather than for the moment? Not many, I think. We often live as if there is no tomorrow, and yet tomorrow always comes. My desire in this book is to help you learn to seize each day and use your will to choose God's will. Use the day to represent God well and to prepare to live in His presence forever.

How can you use today as a time to prepare for eternity?

_____

_____

_____

_____

How would you live your life differently if you knew for sure that Jesus was returning in one week?

_____

_____

_____

_____

What prevents you from living like that now?

_____

_____

However, no one knows the day or hour when these things will happen, not even the angels in heaven or the Son Himself. Only the Father knows.

Matthew 24:36 (NLT)

Read I Corinthians 3:10–14.

What do these verses say about our work and rewards?

_____

_____

Are you living today to receive rewards tomorrow? Explain.

_____

_____

Go!

Assess yourself and answer the following questions:

Are you living carefully? How?

_____

_____

What kind of attitudes and character traits are you clinging to that God doesn't approve of?

_____

_____

How much of your time are you wasting living selfishly instead of loving and serving others and trusting God to take care of you?

_____

_____

_____

_____

It is important to live with an eternal mind-set. If our actions, our attitudes, and our ambitions are carried out with an eternal mind-set rather than a temporal one, we are certain to accomplish bigger and better things for God and the growth of His Kingdom. When we speak of God's Kingdom growing, we are referring to souls being added to it. The salvation of the lost is the important thing on God's agenda, and we have the privilege of being His personal representatives in the earth—God making His appeal to the lost through us.

Look up II Corinthians 5:20, NLT, and fill in the missing words.

So we are Christ's _____; God is making his _____ through _____. We speak for _____ when we plead, "Come _____ to _____!"

How are you pointing people to (or back to) God? What do your words say? What do your actions say?

_____

_____

_____

_____

God gives life meaning! He is everything that is important, and I am excited about spending my time preparing to see Him face-to-face and to live in His presence for all of eternity. The pursuit of God and His will is truly the most noble journey that any of us can undertake.

Spend some time thinking about eternity. Journal your thoughts and what you look forward to.

_____

_____

_____

Get excited about the future and the time we have to prepare to see God face-to-face.

Remember

When talking about seizing the day and living life "on purpose," it is important to live with an eternal mind-set. It is easy to get so caught up in the realities of daily living that we forget the most important reality of all: this world is not our home.

I heard a voice thunder from the Throne: "Look! Look! God has moved into the neighborhood, making his home with men and women! They're his people, he's their God. He'll wipe every tear from their eyes. Death is gone for good—tears gone, crying gone, pain gone—all the first order of things gone." The Enthroned continued, "Look! I'm making everything new. Write it all down—each word dependable and accurate."

Revelation 21:3–5 (MSG)

The Reward of Right Choices

Before you begin, read chapter 4 in *Seize the Day*.

Get Ready...

Review how your perspective has changed now that you have been reminded to live with an eternal mind-set. Journal about any changes you see in your attitude, prayer life, actions, and so on.

_____

_____

_____

Read the opening quote, Deuteronomy 30:19, in several Bible versions. Also read verse 20. Describe how you see "life" as the choice you've made.

_____

_____

_____

Get Set...

We make a lot of choices in a day. Take some time to think of all the choices you've made already today. List them below.

_____

_____

_____

_____

Now go back and review your list. This time, think of what dictated that choice: your emotions, other people, circumstances, the culture we live in, or something else. Circle all the choices you made with your emotions; underline all the choices you made because of other people; draw a dotted line under the choices you made because of circumstances; place a check mark next to the choices you made because of culture; and highlight the choices you made for other reasons.

We need to learn how to make choices that will give us the results we want. It is clear in Scripture that God desires we have a life of fruitfulness, peace, and joy, but we won't have it unless we make choices that are wise.

Review your list of choices and write how you'd like to have handled them had you been thinking of the future. Some may stay the same, but choose wisely how you would change others.

_____

_____

_____

One of the ways we use the authority God has given us is by exercising our freedom of choice in a way that will give us an end result we will be happy with. If we don't make our own decisions, then someone else or something else will decide for us.

Read the story on page 36 about President Ronald Reagan's lesson on making his own choices. Do you agree with the message the cobbler gave Reagan? Explain.

_____

_____

_____

How can the cobbler's message remind you to make your own choices—and to choose wisely?

_____

_____

_____

Spending your time wisely is essential to living your life to the fullest. Think about how you spent your time today or yesterday (if you are completing this exercise in the morning). Write down what you did during each time slot.

8 a.m. (or earlier)

_____

9 a.m.

_____

10 a.m.

_____

11 a.m.

_____

Noon

_____

1 p.m.

_____

2 p.m.

_____

3 p.m.

_____

4 p.m.

_____

5 p.m.

_____

6 p.m.

_____

7 p.m.

_____

8 p.m.

_____

9 p.m.

_____

10 p.m. (and later)

_____

Circle the activities you did that made you feel satisfied; underline the ones you did that made you feel like you were wasting time.

Do you begin your day with God? Why or why not?

_____

_____

_____

Think about ways you can begin your day with God, or enhance the time you already spend with God in the morning. Write some thoughts below.

_____

_____

_____

If we submit our day to the Lord, instead of just planning it on our own, He can work through our thoughts, causing them to be in agreement with His will. We may think we have had a great idea, but it is actually because God has placed the idea in us.

Go!

Read about how I planned my day on page 40. Do you get any ideas about how you can plan your days better? Write them below.

_____

_____

_____

Planning your day and managing your time doesn't mean that you have to work all the time, but you do need to do what you do on purpose! Even if I decide to lie on the couch all day and watch movies, I should do it because I planned to do it, and not because I was cleaning house and saw the couch, lay down, and turned on the television and stayed there all day while thinking, "I should not be doing this."

How do you feel about planning your day? What hinders you from purposefully thinking about what you will do each day?

_____

_____

_____

The fact that I planned my day doesn't mean everything will go exactly the way I planned, but at least I have a direction and a purpose in mind. People full of purpose make the most of the time and talents God has given them.

Each day is different and presents different responsibilities and challenges, so we get to plan each one accordingly. Some days I may work all day, other days I may be with family and friends all day. Planning variety into our schedules is very important if we don't want to get bored with life.

How often do you schedule time to relax and enjoy yourself (not just work)?

_____

_____

How can you add in more time for relaxation and enjoyment if you need more?

_____

_____

Part of becoming an "on-purpose" person is developing an ability to schedule your life in such a way that you are well balanced in all areas. That is why when I plan my day, I almost always schedule time for relaxation and enjoyment as well as work.

You will enjoy your life much more if you take proper time for you! You are not being selfish if you take care of yourself, because the best gift you can give your family and friends is a healthy you.

Read the following scriptures from several Bible translations and write what they say to you about planning your day to live on purpose.

Proverbs 16:9

_____

_____

Proverbs 16:3

_____

_____

Psalm 118:24

_____

_____

Remember

The best choice you can make each day is to begin that day spending time with God.

Today I have given you the choice between life and death, between blessings and curses. Now I call on heaven and earth to witness the choice you make. Oh, that you would choose life, so that you and your descendants might live! You can make this choice by loving the Lord your God, obeying him, and committing yourself firmly to him. This is the key to your life. And if you love and obey the Lord, you will live long in the land the Lord swore to give your ancestors Abraham, Isaac, and Jacob.

Deuteronomy 30:19–20 (NLT)

Where Did All the Time Go?

Before you begin, read chapter 5 in *Seize the Day*.

Get Ready...

Since completing the previous chapter, have you been more consistent in starting your day with God and planning your day in the morning? Write down some observations.

_____

_____

_____

Read the opening scripture, Psalm 39:4, from several translations. Journal your thoughts on time: Do you believe your life is fleeting? Do you think time flies? Why?

_____

_____

_____

Get Set…

How well do you treat each day God gives you as a present, unwrapping the gift carefully, cherishing it, and using it fully and wisely? How can you cherish each day more?

_____

_____

_____

Write down the scripture from Ephesians 5:15–17. Read several translations and choose the one you understand best.

_____

_____

_____

Now review the eight points I list for these verses on page 45. Find each point in the verses, underlining the part that applies to the point. Then write the corresponding number next to the verse.

Commit the verses to memory or write them on your screen saver on your computer or phone (or write them on a piece of paper and keep them visible). Review the verses often.

Take time to think about the following questions. Dig deep and answer them honestly and thoroughly to get the most you can from them.

Am I making the most of my time?

_____

_____

_____

Am I firmly holding on to God's will for my life and refusing to let anything steal it?

_____

_____

_____

Am I living life on purpose, or letting circumstances and people control my destiny?

_____

_____

_____

Am I satisfied with my choices, at least most of the time?

_____

_____

_____

How often do I say, "I don't know where my time goes"?

_____

_____

_____

Am I seizing each day God gives me, and making the most of it?

_____

_____

_____

I have come to the conclusion that I have a responsibility to know where my time goes and to slow down long enough to inventory what I am doing with it, and to make sure it is what I really want to do.

Have you taken responsibility for where your time goes by regularly doing an inventory? What have you discovered?

_____

_____

I doubt that any day goes by that I stay on track all day and don't waste any time. We are humans with inherent weaknesses, but we can improve and grow if we pray and confront areas in our lives that are out of order.

Go!

Read Lamentations 3:23 in several translations. What imagery comes to mind when you think of brand-new mercies every day? Draw a picture below. Spend time reflecting on the fact that God gives us new mercies each and every day.

_____

_____

_____

Choose one of the exercises I recommend on page 48 to inventory your time.

If you find yourself trying to accomplish too much in a day, choose one goal or one thing to accomplish each day. Celebrate your accomplishment at the end of each day.

Or, review your day at the end of each day. Ask yourself where you lost focus or where things went off track. Determine to learn from your mistake. *When you do fail or make mistakes, the best thing to do is to admit them and let them be a tutor for your future. Our mistakes can be valuable if we learn from them.*

Which exercise will you choose to do? Write your plan to execute it below.

_____

_____

_____

Think about the statement I make on page 49: *Time cannot be stored up and used later. Each day we spend our time, and once it is spent we cannot get it back. If we purchase something with money and we aren't happy with it, we can usually take it back to where we purchased it and get our money back or exchange it for something else, but time is not like that. Once it is gone, it cannot ever be regained, and that is why we seriously need to use our time wisely! We want to invest our time, not waste it.*

What do you think about these statements? How can they stimulate you to be a better steward of your time?

_____

_____

_____

_____

Create a pie chart showing how you think you spend your time. Use categories such as caring for yourself, worship, caring for spouse, caring for children, caring for parents or others, work, cleaning the house.

Now draw how you'd like your chart to look—how you would like to spend your time.

Your life is yours and you can take charge of it. Your time is yours and you can put it into God's will for your life. Your schedule is yours; if you don't like it, remember that you made it, and only you can change it.

Making changes in your life often takes time. If a huge ship were going in the wrong direction, it would take some strategy and time to turn it completely around. It is the same way with a life that is going in the wrong direction. Don't be impatient, but be committed to finding out and firmly grasping the Lord's will for your life.

Ask yourself if you are committed to the time it takes to make changes in your life to live more purposefully. Write your thoughts.

_____

_____

_____

Fill in the blanks for Matthew 11:28–29, NLT.

Then _____ said, "Come to me, all of you who are _____ and carry heavy _____, and I will give you _____. Take my _____ upon you. Let me _____ you, because I am humble and _____ at heart, and you will find _____ for your souls.

Read it in several versions, including the one I've written in the book. How does reading this verse make you feel? What do you need to do to find rest?

_____

_____

_____

When you can't do it all, you should choose the best thing for the present time.

How does this work in your life? Recall a time when you had to choose what was best for the time. How did things work out?

_____

_____

How can you practice choosing what is best for the present time when you have too much to do?

_____

_____

_____

What are some other ways you can handle having too much to do?

_____

_____

_____

Remember

Regardless of how much you get done, there is always something left to do, so celebrate what you did accomplish and get up the next day and begin again.

> *For everything there is a season,*
> *a time for every activity under heaven.*
> *A time to be born and a time to die.*
> *A time to plant and a time to harvest....*

Yet God has made everything beautiful for its own time. He has planted eternity in the human heart, but even so, people cannot see the whole scope of God's work from beginning to end.

Ecclesiastes 3:1–2, 11 (NLT)

Ways to Avoid Wasting Your Time

Before you begin, read chapter 6 in *Seize the Day*.

Get Ready...

Now that you've completed exercises about how you spend the time in your day, what have you done differently? What have been the results?

_____

_____

_____

Read the opening scripture, Ephesians 5:16, in several translations. What does the verse say to you?

_____

_____

Get Set...

Take a self-evaluation test to determine how you might be wasting time. Use the questions and statements I list on pages 54–55.

1. How often do you complain about your busy schedule? What do you say?

_____

_____

2. Do you think you can do everything and do it well? Explain.

_____

_____

_____

3. What do you let hijack your time?

_____

_____

_____

4. Are you just busy, or are you productive? How do you differentiate between the two?

_____

_____

_____

5. Are you able to stay focused on what you really want to do?

_____

_____

_____

6. Do you spend more time talking about things you need to get done than actually doing them? Explain.

_____

_____

_____

7. Do you buy time by getting less sleep and then lose time because you are tired? Explain.

_____

_____

_____

8. How often do you make mistakes because you are in a hurry? Share an example.

_____

_____

_____

9. How often do you have to repair something because you didn't want to spend the money to do it right to begin with? Share an example.

_____

_____

_____

10. Do you deal with little problems in order to prevent them from becoming big problems? Explain.

_____

_____

_____

Go!

The Fixes

(It's a good idea to read each section, but focus on the issues you identified in your self-assessment.)

Complaining

If you are a complainer, have you considered an action plan to change things? Or do you want to continue to complain about the same situation? What can you do today to begin to fix your busy schedule?

_____

_____

_____

Complaining is useless and changes nothing. Prayer, combined with taking action according to God's guidance, is the only answer to any problem we have. God's Word teaches us not to worry and to cast our care, but it never says we are to cast our responsibility.

Read I Peter 5:7 from several translations. Write down the version you understand best. Consider committing it to memory.

_____

_____

_____

Read I Thessalonians 5:18 from several translations. Write down the version you understand best. Consider committing it to memory.

_____

_____

_____

Does your plan combine prayer, thanksgiving, and action? If not, reevaluate it and edit your plan below.

_____

_____

_____

Priorities

List, in order of importance, what is important to you.

_____

_____

_____

_____

_____

_____

_____

_____

Keeping those priorities in mind, how can you better plan your day to make sure you are taking care of what's most important to you first?

We have to have the ability to know which things in our lives are the most important to us and then be sure that we make time for them. If we don't, we will spend our lives doing what is urgent rather than what is important. Our time belongs to us, and we can prioritize it wisely if we truly want to.

How will you arrange your schedule to be more in line with your priorities? How can reminding yourself of your priorities help you choose wisely throughout the day?

_____

_____

_____

If everything is a priority to us, then nothing is a priority, and we live confused and frustrated lives. Some people try to do everything, so they do nothing really well. Are you able to focus on what is truly important and always make sure you give those things the attention they deserve? If not, that is a good place *to begin becoming an "on-purpose" person who is able to seize the day! At our ministry we often say, "Be sure the benefit we reap from a project equals the time put into it."*

Time Hijackers

What sucks up your time and needs to be placed on your "no fly" list? Pay attention to your time over the next week and see what takes you away from doing what is important to you.

_____

_____

_____

Consider how much time you spend engaging with modern technology: cell phones, social media, e-mail, and so on. How can you handle these modern conveniences differently so that your time is not hijacked in areas on which you do not intend to focus?

_____

_____

_____

Do you have any people who hijack your time (intentionally or unintentionally)? How can you handle their interruptions (or stop their interruptions) so you can focus on your priorities?

_____

_____

_____

How often do unplanned or unexpected interruptions hijack your time? How can you leave some room in your schedule for the unexpected?

_____

_____

_____

Are you a culprit in wasting your own time? What other things can get you off track and cause you to waste time?

_____

_____

_____

To be a person who lives life "on purpose," we will have to be relentless in dealing with things that get us off the track we want to be on. The more we do it, the easier it will become, but let me be clear that living the life you truly want to live will be something you will have to be firm about. Not everyone may understand your determination, but you will be the one who will accomplish great things instead of living with regrets over what you wish you had done with your life.

Buying Time

If you forgo sleep to get more time, how do you feel when working—energized or tired? Do you see how sacrificing your rest and well-being actually takes away from productivity? Explain.

_____

_____

_____

How can you fix the problem of using less sleep to get "more" done?

_____

_____

_____

I have come to a point in my life where I realize one of my greatest needs is energy! When I am tired or don't feel well, it affects every area of my life adversely. I no longer buy time by giving up sleep or rushing continually, because I have learned the hard way that I always lose time in the end. It may be visits to the doctor, or making unnecessary mistakes because I am tired, but it will always cost me eventually.

Do you rush through projects to buy more time but spend even more time fixing mistakes? Explain.

_____

_____

_____

What can you do to stop rushing through projects and paying the price of fixing mistakes?

_____

_____

_____

Doing a thing right or in an excellent manner always takes more time than merely doing it quickly just to get it done and check it off of our list. Some personality types just want every project off their list, and they often make mistakes in judgment because they don't wait for wisdom. I make quick decisions and sometimes I cost myself time because I didn't think a thing all the way through.

Frugal, Not Foolish

How often do you find yourself spending more money on repairs because you didn't want to spend money up front? Do you consider the long-term effect of your decisions or just short-term? How can you plan better?

_____

_____

_____

I am prudent, but I really try not to be foolish. My time is valuable; as they often say, "Time is money." If you have not realized yet that your time is valuable, I suggest you think it over, because time may be one of the most valuable things you have.

Compromises

Have you ever compromised on something—didn't spend time, money, or effort on a "small issue"—but soon found out you had to spend more time, money, or effort because the small issue became larger? Explain.

_____

_____

_____

We often compromise in order to get what we want when we want it, or in order not to have to spend time on something we don't want to spend it on, but compromise always costs us in the long run.

Sometimes we don't do a thing just because we don't want to and for no other reason. It is, of course, our privilege to choose, but then we should not complain if what we didn't do turns into something more for us to do eventually.

It is wise to find the ways we waste time and ruthlessly eliminate them from our life. Do today what you will be happy with tomorrow, and then tomorrow you won't regret what you didn't do today!

What changes will you make today to be happy tomorrow?

_____

_____

_____

Go!

In order to seize the day, it is important to stay on task in your life. Don't let unnecessary interruptions steal your time.

> Lazy people don't even cook the game they catch, but the diligent make use of everything they find. The way of the godly leads to life; that path does not lead to death.
>
> Proverbs 12:27–28 (NLT)

We Only Get One Life

Before you begin, read chapter 7 in *Seize the Day*.

Get Ready...

Now that you've evaluated your life for time wasters and developed action plans, have you noticed a difference in how you seize the day? Explain.

_____

_____

_____

Read the opening quote, Acts 20:24, from several versions, including the paraphrased one in *Seize the Day*. How does this verse remind you to seize the day?

_____

_____

_____

Write "I will run my race to the end!" on a notecard and display it in a place you will see it often; you could also make it the screen saver for your phone or computer.

Get Set…

If you were asked to give an account of your life today, what would you say? Write it below.

_____

_____

_____

It is good to remember that we only have one life to live and then we will come face-to-face with God, who will ask us to give an account for ourselves. That is why Paul said in Romans 14:12, "And so each of us shall give an account of himself [give an answer in reference to judgment] to God."

This is not intended to frighten us, but to urge us to realize that eventually the time we have been given will run out and we will be asked to give an account of what we have done with it. This scripture doesn't frighten me, but it does urge me to be sober-minded about my life and use it to please God.

Since "the wise man always lets his mistakes educate him," what have you learned from the time you may have wasted in the past? What will you do differently to live your life on purpose?

_____

_____

_____

In this chapter, I talk about another thing that may possibly be hijacking your time: your emotions. Take a deep breath, ask God to reveal to you internal issues you need to deal with, and honestly assess yourself by answering the following questions:

Do you feel guilty about anything? (Think about your past or any feelings of regret you may have.) Write about them here.

_____

_____

_____

Are you fearful about something? How do you feel about the future?

_____

_____

_____

What do you worry about most?

_____

_____

_____

Are you anxious about anything? Do you have peace, or are you constantly thinking about something?

_____

_____

_____

Do you often wish you had something someone has? Or do you often wish you were a different person?

_____

_____

_____

Do you constantly want more (not to accomplish goals, but to have more), or are you content with what you have? Explain.

_____

_____

_____

Do you think ill of others who may have more—or something different—than you? Explain.

_____

_____

_____

Do you find it hard to forgive others—for big and small offenses? Explain.

_____

_____

_____

Are you down on yourself, often feeling sorry for yourself and your circumstances? Explain.

_____

_____

_____

If we want to seize the day, we must be prepared to seize negative emotions that will rob us of the day. Emotions that we don't want may visit us quite suddenly, without an invitation from us. All it takes is for someone to swoop in front of us and take the parking place we have been waiting for at the mall, and we get a visit from anger. Or for someone we work with to get the promotion that we believe we deserve more than they do, and we get a visit from jealousy, resentment, and anger.

Because we never know on any given day what our circumstances may be, and because we cannot control the actions of other people, we are in danger every day of wasting time on negative, useless emotions. It is quite possible that there are more people in the world right now who are either experiencing some of these emotions or are angry about one thing or another than there are those who are totally at peace.

Go!

It's time to seize your emotions and stop them from hijacking your time and peace.

Read Matthew 5:9 from several versions of the Bible.

What does it mean to be a part of God's family (a son or daughter)?

Sons have a degree of maturity. We don't expect anything other than unbridled emotions from babies and children, but we do expect more than that from our grown sons and daughters, and so does God.

Read Proverbs 25:28. What type of person is like a broken city without boundaries or walls? Journal about the comparison.

I have found it very helpful to resist negative, unwanted emotions at their onset. When something happens that causes unwanted emotions to rise up within you, subdue them. If you let the emotion lead, you are headed for trouble. Name the emotion and say, "You're not welcome," and then start talking to yourself. For example: If I were to hear of a ministry opportunity a friend had received and it was one I had always dreamed of, I might get a visit from jealousy and envy. As soon as I noticed it, I should say, "Jealousy and envy, you are not welcome here!" Then I can have a talk with myself, saying, "Joyce, you are so blessed that it would be ridiculous for you to be jealous of anyone. God has a unique plan for each of us, and Joyce, you have done things that others have never done, and some of them will do things you will never do." I always find when I do this that my emotions calm down and I can behave properly.

What issues did you identify with in the self-assessment? Find two or three and write a script to "talk yourself off the ledge" when you encounter that emotion.

_____

_____

_____

_____

_____

_____

Match the scripture reference with the main theme of the scriptures that can help with some internal emotion.

God loves us and will do what is best for us; there's no need to fear.	Romans 12:21
Use good to overcome evil.	Isaiah 53:5–6
Forgiveness is a cycle.	I John 4:18
God takes care of you—don't worry.	Matthew 6:33–34
God gives us guilt-free living in Jesus.	Matthew 6:15

Your time is valuable, so don't waste any of it on negative, useless emotions that do nothing but make you miserable.

Remember

Your life doesn't have to be run by your emotions. You can make the decision to control your emotions instead of them controlling you.

In order to enjoy your life, it is important to learn to be content. God wants us to be content with what we have, ask Him for what we want and need, and trust that He will provide it at the right time.

The thief's purpose is to steal and kill and destroy. My purpose is to give them a rich and satisfying life.

John 10:10 (NLT)

Determination

Before you begin, read chapter 8 in *Seize the Day*.

Get Ready…

Have you noticed a difference in how you handle your emotions so they don't hijack your time? Explain.

_____

_____

_____

Read the opening quote about determination. Do you agree with the quote? Does it encourage you to be more determined? Explain.

_____

_____

_____

Consider writing the quote in a place you will see often.

Get Set…

Determined people are rare, but nothing in the world can take the place of determination and persistence. Talent doesn't take its place, education doesn't take its place, and neither does any level of genius. The world is filled with common men and women who have done uncommon things, but all of them had determination. I am of the opinion that nothing good happens by accident.

Determination triumphs over any deficit we can name. Anyone who wants to have determination can have it. It doesn't belong to a privileged few. You might say, "Well, I am just not aggressive," but making progress in life does not require a naturally aggressive personality. It simply requires that you are determined to make your life count.

Using the scale below, how determined do you think you are?

Not very determined at all	Somewhat determined	Determined some of the time	Very determined

Journal about how determined you are and how this impacts your life.

_____

_____

_____

_____

How is the Holy Spirit our greatest source of strength and power? How does He enable you to overcome obstacles? Share a time when you relied on the Holy Spirit and you gained strength.

_____

_____

_____

If you have very little determination and tend to give up easily, then at least begin making a change by praying that God will work determination in you. Believe that He has heard and answered you, and then step out in faith, trusting that the feelings you desire will come as you go forward. The excuse that we don't feel like doing a thing that is right is a pitiful excuse. I doubt seriously that Jesus "felt" like going to the cross and dying for the sins of mankind, but He did it relying on something much deeper than His feelings. He relied on the power of God to enable Him, and looked forward to the joy that was on the other side of the pain.

Read Romans 8:26–27 from several translations. How does the Holy Spirit help us, according to these verses?

_____

_____   _____

_____

Look up II Corinthians 5:17 from several translations. Fill in the missing words according to the New Century Version.

If _____ belongs to _____, there is a new creation. The old things have _____; everything is made _____!

Have you accepted Christ and accepted yourself as a new creation? Explain.

_____

_____

_____

Write II Corinthians 5:17 in your own words. Use it to help you overcome the past or any negative things you feel about yourself. Remind yourself that you are new and the old has no influence on you.

_____

_____

Read I Corinthians 1:9 from several translations and write a prayer thanking God for His faithfulness.

_____

_____

_____

Go!

It is very difficult for us to believe what we cannot see or feel, but faith is the assurance of what we cannot see. We take the promises of God as fact, and we decide to live according to them. I cannot see gravity, but I believe in it because I am not floating in the air right now. Sitting in my home today, looking out my window, I cannot see the wind, but I am aware that it is blowing because I see the trees moving. We cannot see God, but we can see the things He does in our lives, and even if those things are small, they encourage us to believe for better things. Do you see the things that God has done in your life, or do you stay busy seeing what He has not done yet? If you do that, you will become quickly discouraged and give up. Take time every day to thank God for every tiny thing He has provided for you, and as you do it will increase your faith. Even in the midst of great difficulty, we can continue thanking God, believing that He can and will work good out of it.

List some of the things God has done for you in the past. Keep reminding yourself of God's goodness and faithfulness—even during difficult times.

_____

_____

_____

Read the short book of Ruth and answer the following questions:

1. How did Ruth's determination help her change her circumstance?

    _____

    _____

2. How did Ruth's life change after she committed to helping her mother-in-law?

    _____

    _____

3. What can you use from Ruth's story to be more determined?

    _____

    _____

If we don't disrespect the handfuls God leaves us on purpose, we will some-day be the one leaving handfuls for others. God will bless you and make you a blessing!

Find a scripture that reminds you to keep going when life is hard. Write it below and commit it to memory.

_____

_____

_____

We will go through hard things, and when we do, we can determine not to give up, but to press through. We can do so with a thankful heart and a good attitude, trusting God every step of the way.

Find a scripture that reminds you to hope and wait in God—even when it feels like God is moving slowly. Write it below and commit it to memory (or keep it in a place where you will see it often).

_____

_____

_____

Focusing on what we want is the thing that makes waiting so difficult. We can choose instead to focus on God and use the extra time we have while waiting to grow in Him. God is good, and He will not withhold anything good from us unless it is for a good reason. I spent years frustrated because my ministry grew so pitifully slowly, and at times I even felt that it went backward for a season. I could not understand why God wasn't doing what I was asking Him to do. No matter what I did, God didn't move any faster.

Of course, now I look back and understand all too well that I wanted something that I was not spiritually mature enough to have, and God in His mercy withheld it. The attitude I had while waiting was in itself proof that I wasn't ready for more. Why should God ever give us "more" of anything if we are not thankful for the things He has already given us, no matter how small they are? Always remember that a delay is not a denial, and when God seems slow, be determined to stand firm.

Find a scripture that can comfort you when you feel lonely. Write it below.

_____

_____

_____

The pain we endure at various seasons in life is temporary, and it is very important to remember that when we are going through it. "This too shall pass" is one of my favorite sayings. The sun always shines after the storm!

No matter what might be causing us to want to give up, we can be determined to press on. If we give up, it will only mean we have to start again at another time. We'll still need to face what we ran from the first time!

Remember

Determination helps you practice good habits until they become a natural part of your life.

> Now faith is the substance of things hoped for, the evidence of things not seen.
>
> Hebrews 11:1 (KJV)

Seize the Day

Before you get started, read chapter 9 in *Seize the Day*.

Get Ready…

Have you noticed that you are more determined to seize the day and live your life on purpose after completing the previous chapter? Explain.

_____

_____

Read the opening quote by Mother Teresa. How does it apply to seizing the day?

_____

_____

_____

What does the word *seize* mean to you? How does it apply to living life on purpose?

_____

_____

_____

Get Set...

What's your general attitude when you wake up each morning? Have you learned to wake up ready to seize the day? Explain.

_____

_____

Far too many people are inactive, and they wait for something to fall into their laps—they end up waiting until it is too late. They live unsatisfied and unproductive lives simply because they don't wake up each day ready to seize the day and make the most out of it.

Are you waiting for something to fall in your lap, or are you actively trying to seize each day? Explain.

_____

_____

Ask yourself if the devil has stolen anything from you. (Write notes next to each item that the devil has stolen from you.) Has the devil stolen:

Your confidence?

_____

_____

Your courage?

_____

_____

Your identity?

_____

_____

Your energy?

_____

_____

Your zeal?

_____

_____

Your enthusiasm for life?

_____

_____

Your peace?

_____

_____

Your joy?

_____

_____

Your right standing with God as His child? Do you know who you are in Christ and the privileges your inheritance from Him gives you?

_____

_____

Read the verses on restoration: Zechariah 9:12, Isaiah 61:7, Proverbs 6:31.
Journal how you feel knowing that God can and will restore what the devil has stolen.

_____

_____

_____

When we lack correct knowledge, the devil takes advantage of us, but once we know the truth of God's Word it makes us free. The term "makes us free" doesn't mean that freedom magically happens with no action on our part. The truth we apply to our lives is what will make us free. Just the realization that we don't have to live as victims, but that we actually can wake up and seize the day, is in itself freedom!

Go!

Whether you are a victim or a victor, try the exercise I suggest on pages 88–89. Write what you will say to yourself before you get out of bed each morning.

_____

_____

_____

Be prepared to do this day after day, and you will soon begin to see results. It takes time to renew the mind, so don't be disappointed if you do not get immediate results. It is great if you do get them, but at least be prepared not to give up, and to be determined to keep doing the right thing. Beginning each day with this mind-set helps you get your day started right.

Read Paul's determined statements from several versions of the Bible and journal how they make you feel. Remember that Paul spent much of his time writing while he was in prison. Use him as an example of seizing the day—regardless of your current circumstances.

Read Philippians 3:7–14.

_____

_____

_____

Do you feel like you have the zeal described in the original language of Matthew 11:12? If not, write a prayer asking for help.

_____

_____

_____

As you pray, keep notes of thoughts that may come to mind or ideas you may receive on increasing your zeal.

_____

_____

Focus on Jesus, how much He loves you and what He has done for you. As you receive His love and let it amaze you, you will find yourself wanting to do all that He asks you to do. The development of your personal relationship with God is very important, because it is the foundation for all obedience. Jesus said, "If you [really] love Me, you will keep and obey My commandments" (John 14:15). The apostle John wrote that we love Him because He first loved us (see I John 4:19); therefore, receiving God's love will cause you to love Him in return, and out of that love you will obey Him.

Struggling to do the right thing by willpower alone only helps to a small degree. When we run out of our own strength, which we all do, then we need the power of God (His grace) to bring us through to the finish. Because this book is filled with encouragement for you to be aggressive, active, enthusiastic, passionate, and filled with zeal, it is also important that I warn you of the dangers of "works of the flesh." These are things we try to do in our own effort and strength that can only be done with God's help. "God, help me" is one of the most important prayers we need to pray throughout each day of our lives.

Remember

You can choose an attitude that says, "I will have what belongs to me as a child of God! I will not be cheated! I will seize the day!"

Ask and it will be given to you; seek and you will find; knock and the door will be opened to you. For everyone who asks receives; the one who seeks finds; and to the one who knocks, the door will be opened.

Matthew 7:7–8 (NIV)

Scheduling and Planning

Before you begin, read chapter 10 in *Seize the Day*.

Get Ready...

Can you see how your zeal and determination to seize the day has changed since you started working through this book? Share insights you have received.

_____

_____

Read the opening verse, Psalm 143:8, from several translations. How can this scripture help you to seize each day?

_____

_____

Write your morning prayer below. Remember to start the day off focusing on God, which will give you many benefits and help you to seize the day.

_____

_____

Get Set…

How well do you plan your day before you start? What obstacles do you have to planning?

_____

_____

When we ask God for direction, we probably won't be given a specific outline of what the day should look like, but we can depend on God to guide us as we schedule and plan our day. God has given us common sense and wisdom as gifts, and as a part of our free will, He expects us to use them in daily planning. Planning is simply thinking wisely. It is looking at how much time you have and deciding what you want or need to do with it.

Do you have any unfinished projects that you don't like to think about? How can you plan a schedule to get them done and eliminate the stress they cause?

_____

_____

God helps us in our weaknesses. His strength is actually seen through them. Pray, make a plan, and trust God to help you remember to work your plan!

How often do you allow spontaneous events to take you off plan? Do you think you need more balance between the spontaneous and the planned? Explain.

_____

_____

Think about your responsibilities before you run off and do something spontaneous.

Responsibility, even though it may not always be the most exciting thing, is an important priority.

What method of planning works best for you? (Very systematic planning, less structured planning, broad planning, etc.)

_____

_____

_____

Go!

Is there anything you say you want to do but don't have time to do (like exercising, reading your Bible, etc.)? What plan can you implement to incorporate it into your schedule if it is important to you?

_____

_____

_____

If you don't succeed, remember to try different things, different times, or different approaches.

Give yourself time and room to be imperfect while you're improving.

What are some things you can plan to neglect that will actually help you seize the day (like the telephone, e-mail, social media, etc.)?

_____

_____

_____

The more we are available, the more people depend on us. We can give others some responsibility by simply planning a little neglect. I am not suggesting that we neglect legitimate responsibilities, but we truly don't have to be available to everyone all the time.

Remember

Time management is really self-management. If we don't manage ourselves, our lives can be nothing other than chaotic. Frustrated people usually blame their problems on life, but God doesn't want life to just happen to us, He wants us to subdue and manage it.

Pray, make a plan, and trust God to help you work your plan.

Following Through with Your Plan

Before you begin, read chapter 11 in *Seize the Day*.

Get Ready...

How has planning helped you do things you couldn't find the time to do but deemed important? Share insights and remember that it may take a long time to see results, but keep trying.

_____

_____

_____

Read the opening quote by Mary Kay Ash, founder of Mary Kay Cosmetics. Write your thoughts on the quote. Do you believe follow-through is needed to excel and to learn to seize the day?

_____

_____

_____

Assess yourself. How good are you at following through with what you have planned to do?

I rarely follow through	I am not very good at following through	I am okay at following through	I follow through most of the time	I always follow through

Get Set…

Adjust your attitude on follow-through by adopting my three ways to accomplish your goals.

1. Have a "Today is the Day" Attitude

Perhaps you have heard the saying, "The best time to do what needs to be done is now," and that is certainly true. Whether it is paying the bills that are due or picking up the little piece of paper you dropped on the floor—the best time is now! The ability to move oneself to immediate action in dealing with what needs to be done is the trait of a successful person.

How can you adopt an attitude to provoke immediate action?

_____

_____

_____

We subconsciously think that if we do all the things that need to be done now, we won't have time to do the things we want to do, but that isn't true. We will actually have more time to do those things, and we will be able to do them peacefully, without low-level guilt over our procrastination.

2. Dealing with Interruptions Successfully

Should we become frustrated with those people and things that interrupt us, or should we find ways to protect ourselves when we are doing things we don't want interrupted?

Write down the times when you are interrupted the most. Write down some ways that you can protect yourself from these interruptions.

_____

_____

_____

We cannot expect the rest of the world to stop functioning because we don't want to be interrupted, so why not be proactive and make arrangements to be where your interruptions will be fewer?

How can you avoid interrupting others, particularly in the office?

_____

_____

_____

Too much of anything, even a good thing, always becomes a problem. Use technology, but don't let it run your life, or possibly ruin your life. We may need to multitask occasionally, but we don't have to live that way. Some interruptions are part of everyone's life, but we can learn to manage them better.

3. Count the Cost before Committing

Read Proverbs 12:24, NIV, and fill in the blanks.

_____ hands will rule, but _____ ends in _____ labor.

How does this verse prompt you to be more diligent?

_____

_____

_____

How often do you ask yourself how much time an activity will require before you commit to it?

_____

_____

How often do you evaluate your activities—and their value?

_____

_____

One of the big mistakes an organization or an individual may make is to keep doing something that was valuable at one time but is no longer valuable. Take a fresh look at what you are doing on a regular basis and ask if it is something worth doing.

Go!

Use this time to reevaluate what you spend your time on. Is there anything that once held value to you but now is not worth your time? What can you do to eliminate that activity?

_____

_____

_____

What have you been desiring to do but haven't found the time for in your schedule? Think about how much time you need for the activity. How can you add it to your plans?

_____

_____

_____

Whether you want to build a house, lose weight, get out of debt, get a college degree, clean the closet, or anything else, count the cost! Ask yourself enough questions to be realistic about what it will take to do it; otherwise you will make a plan and then not follow through!

Remember

The best way to correct a bad habit is to form a good habit. Take action instead of procrastinating. Be proactive and make arrangements that will help limit interruptions.

In view of all this, make every effort to respond to God's promises. Supplement your faith with a generous provision of moral excellence, and moral excellence with knowledge, and knowledge with self-control, and self-control with patient endurance, and patient endurance with godliness, and godliness with brotherly affection, and brotherly affection with love for everyone.

II Peter 1:5–7 (NLT)

Organization

Before you begin, read chapter 12 in *Seize the Day*.

Get Ready...

Have you found ways to decrease procrastination and increase follow-through since completing the previous chapter? Share your insights.

_____

_____

_____

Read the opening quote. Do you agree or disagree with its implications? Explain.

_____

_____

_____

Do you think spending time organizing can help you gain more time or lose more time? Why?

_____

_____

_____

Get Set…

We can waste a lot of time going to find things that we need for a project, but, even more importantly, when we break our concentration there is always a temptation to lose focus and waste even more time.

Do you keep the tools you need for your most important activities in one place? How can you better organize those tools so you will have them in one convenient place when you need them?

_____

_____

_____

How has organization saved you time in the past, or how has disorganization cost you time?

_____

_____

_____

Read the scripture Ecclesiastes 5:3 in several different translations. What other words are used for business? How do they apply to being organized?

_____

_____

_____

What do you need to add to make your dreams a reality, or to accomplish a particular goal? How does organization impact your goal?

_____

_____

_____

Dreams come to pass with much business and painful effort. A home is not built on a wish, good parenting must be more than a wish, and good health is more than a wish. Start with a dream and then add the things that will bring it to pass. Organization is one of those things.

Do you feel your home has too much clutter, or have you organized it well? Explain.

_____

_____

_____

Have you considered a plan—a schedule—to begin to rid your house of clutter? How can you start?

_____

_____

_____

The best way to keep things organized is to implement small daily routines that will, over time, result in a better-kept environment. It is also wise to make sure that everyone in the household is doing his or her part. Many parents struggle with this, but the best thing to do is to train children when they are young to pick up after themselves. If you do everything for them when they are little, you will more than likely still be doing it as they get older.

If you think it is already too late, don't just give up. It is never too late for a new beginning in any area of life. Even if you have a problem, don't keep adding to it by continuing the same bad habits that created it to begin with.

Think about some of the things in your home that you can do without, or that you may be hanging on to just because someone gave them to you. What things can you get rid of to make your house or workspace less cluttered so you can be more organized and enjoy what you do have?

_____

_____

_____

How does passing on your resources to others make you a good steward?

_____

_____

_____

God's Word urges us to be prudent (see Proverbs 13:16). Prudence is good management of our resources. We should use the things we have, because if we don't we are wasting them. There is someone somewhere who will use what is merely collecting dust in our homes, so let's pass these items on.

Go...

Read the list of ways organization can improve your life. Next to the ones you need more of in your life, write some thoughts on getting more organized and create a plan.

1. Organization reduces financial stress.

    _____

    _____

    _____

If, due to a lack of organization, you misplace bills, have to pay late fees, and repurchase items that you cannot find, the costs add up quickly. Financial stress is one of the major causes of marital problems. The Bible says that a wise man knows the state of his flocks. For us that means he knows how much money he has and what he is doing with it. He knows when his bills are due, and he pays them early or on time.

2. Organization minimizes personal conflicts.

_____

_____

_____

A disorganized person cannot be depended on to follow through with tasks, and the trust is eroded in a marriage when this happens. We need to be able to depend on those we are in relationships with.

3. Organization increases "me" time.

_____

_____

_____

When we are organized it leaves time to do the things we really enjoy. Like exercise (yes, some people actually like it) or a painting class or reading. However, if we never have time for those things, we soon begin to feel deprived, and that creates resentment. If these feelings are present for a long time, they will eventually create other bad attitudes and problems.

4. Organization helps us have a better diet.

_____

_____

_____

Many people have very poor eating habits and they say they don't have time to prepare the foods that are healthy. They eat a lot of fast food or prepackaged foods that are stripped of a lot of the needed nutrition. They don't even have time to purchase and take vitamins. Is it possible that a little more organization could give us time to be healthier? I think it is entirely possible, and I believe eating well should be a greater priority.

Remember

The best way to keep things organized is to implement small daily routines that will, over time, result in a better-kept environment. Chaos hinders creativity.

All who are prudent act with knowledge, but fools expose their folly.
                                                    Proverbs 13:16 (NIV)

What Are You Living For?

Before you begin, read chapter 13 in *Seize the Day*.

Get Ready...

Now that you have read more about being organized, have you made any changes that you think have saved you time and helped you live more purposefully? Explain.

_____

_____

_____

Read the opening quote by Billy Sunday. Do you agree with the quote? Why or why not?

_____

_____

_____

Which one do you think you have more of: purpose or talent? Explain.

_____

_____

_____

Get Set...

You are here because God wants you! You are important to Him, and you fit into His purposes. You are not an accident. You are personally designed by the hand of God and have been given abilities that you are to use in the service of God and man.

Have you accepted yourself for who you are and who you were designed to be, or are you comparing yourself to others or wondering why you were created? Explain.

_____

_____

_____

One of our downfalls is that we compare ourselves, and what we can or cannot do, with other people. That is a huge mistake. God will never help you be anyone other than you! I think self-acceptance is vital if we intend to go on to find our purpose in life. In addition to loving God, fellowshipping with Him, and becoming a disciple of Jesus who is being molded into His image, we each have a part to play in the plan of God for the redemption of man.

Write what you are good at:

_____

_____

_____

Write what interests you:

_____

_____

_____

Write what makes you unique:

_____

_____

_____

Can you honestly say, "I like myself, and I love myself with the love of God"? If not, what keeps you from fully believing this?

_____

_____

Read Psalm 139:13–16 from The Message paraphrase of the Bible and fill in the blanks.

> Oh yes, you shaped _____ first _____, then out;
> you formed me in my mother's womb.
> I thank you, High God—you're breathtaking!
> Body and soul, I am _____ made!
> I worship in adoration—what a _____!
> You know me inside and out,
> you know every _____ in my body;
> You know exactly how I was _____, bit by bit,
> how I was sculpted from nothing into _____.
> Like an open book, you watched me grow from conception to birth;
> all the _____ of my life were spread out before you,
> The days of my life all _____
> before I'd even lived one day.

Journal about how these verses make you feel. Are there any parts of the verses that you struggle to believe? Are there any parts that make you excited and more determined to live your life with purpose? Explain.

_____

Just because I may not be what I would have liked does not mean that I am not exactly what God wanted me to be. I may not be behaving exactly the way He would like me to, but our behavior improves as we learn the Word of God and develop a strong relationship with Him. God loves us while we are changing just as much as He will once we have changed!

One of the best ways that you can stop wasting time is to accept yourself as God designed you this very moment. Don't ever fight against yourself again. Say, "I am what I am, and I cannot do anything God has not designed me to do—but I can do everything He has purposed for me. I accept myself as God's creation. He loves me and has a purpose for my life." Even if you don't know what that purpose is yet, this will help you get on your way to discovering it.

Go!

What are some purposes for which you think you were created?

_____

_____

How were you prepared—or are currently being prepared—for these purposes?

_____

_____

Write a prayer asking God to guide you into His purposes for your life.

_____

_____

_____

Now write action steps that will help you bloom where you are.

_____

_____

_____

How can you be available for God's assignment at any time?

_____

_____

_____

Do you believe that money and fame alone will not provide satisfaction? Explain what you think will provide satisfaction.

_____

_____

_____

How can you adjust your priorities to put your energy into the things that truly matter?

_____

_____

_____

Read Proverbs 23:5 from several translations. Do you believe that wealth can disappear so quickly? Explain. How does this help you find something that matters more than money?

_____

_____

_____

If the purpose of life is to be useful, how purposefully are you living? What changes can you make to be more useful or helpful to others?

_____

_____

_____

Ask yourself the questions I pose on page 136:

Are you living to make a difference?

_____

_____

_____

Do you want the world to miss you when you are gone? Explain.

_____

_____

_____

How do you want to be remembered? Try writing a portion of your obituary below. How would you like it to read?

_____

_____

_____

Constantly ask yourself what John W. Gardner asks: *What have you done that you believe in and you are proud of?*

I think the only people we truly remember in life are those who used their lives to help or bless others in some way. I doubt that there is any truly important reason we can find to live merely for ourselves. If we are not living our lives to make someone else's better, then we are not really living at all. Therefore, let me ask one final time: What are you living for?

Remember

Each one of us must decide for ourselves what we want to do with the one life that we have.

> You made all the delicate, inner parts of my body and knit me together in my mother's womb. Thank you for making me so wonderfully complex! Your workmanship is marvelous—how well I know it.
>
> Psalm 139:13–14 (NLT)

Being an "On-Purpose" Person

Before you begin, read chapter 14 in *Seize the Day*.

Get Ready...

Have you been living your life with more purpose since completing several chapters in this book? Share.

_____

_____

_____

Describe what you think an on-purpose person looks like.

_____

_____

_____

Compare your description to the passage about Jesus in Luke 4:42–43.

_____

_____

_____

Get Set...

Read the passage in Luke 4:1–13 in which Satan tried to tempt Jesus to move away from His divine purpose.

Why do you think the devil didn't want Jesus to accomplish His purpose?

_____

_____

_____

How did Jesus resist the temptations set forth by the devil?

_____

_____

_____

How can you find comfort and strength in resisting temptation when you realize that Jesus was also tempted to walk away (or put aside) His purpose?

_____

_____

_____

Now read Matthew 16:21–28 from several translations of the Bible.

Peter was a follower of Jesus, yet he tried to stop Jesus from fulfilling his purpose. Why do you think people closest to us may try to stop us from living out our purpose?

_____

_____

_____

What can you take from Peter and Jesus' conversation to help you deal with those close to you who may not want you to fulfill your purpose?

_____

_____

_____

It is very clear in Scripture that in the midst of opposition we must determine whether we will choose to please God or people as we travel through life. If we make the right choice now, we will avoid living with regrets later on.

Go!

To be passionate means to be compelled to do a thing by strong, intense feelings. I mentioned that I have pursued one main purpose with passion. But in order to have passion we must enjoy what we do.

What are you passionate about? How can that lead to your purpose?

_____

_____

_____

What are you good at? How might that lead to your purpose?

_____

_____

_____

It makes me sad to watch people go through life miserable because they deeply dislike what they are doing. Don't be afraid to make a change, or take a risk. You never know what you may find on the other side of what you think is "safe." Find something that you can be committed to and do it with all of your heart.

Passion keeps us going even in times when we want to give up. Building anything requires a lot of courage and sacrifice, and there are times when we wonder if it is worth it. If we have true passion, we cannot quit even if we want to. Passion takes us across the finish line of our race in life.

How can thinking about the things you are passionate about—and doing them—create enthusiasm for your day?

_____

_____

_____

A positive mind leads to an energetic, enthusiastic life!

Remember

Jesus is the best example to follow as you strive to live an "on-purpose" life.

> Imitate God, therefore, in everything you do, because you are his dear children. Live a life filled with love, following the example of Christ. He loved us and offered himself as a sacrifice for us, a pleasing aroma to God.
>
> Ephesians 5:1–2 (NLT)

Activity and Passivity

Before you begin, read chapter 15 in *Seize the Day*.

Get Ready...

How has remembering Jesus' example of living out His purpose helped you to press toward living your purpose? Share.

_____

_____

_____

Read the opening scripture, Jeremiah 1:12. Do you see God as alert and active? Explain.

_____

_____

_____

Do you see yourself as alert and active? Explain.

_____

_____

_____

Get Set...

Passivity is non-action or non-resistance. The passive person is led by feelings more than by following the leading of the Holy Spirit. Passive people have free will, or the power of choice, but they don't use it, and the problems their passivity leads to are too great to be calculated accurately. One definition of passivity that I have heard is "receiving suffering without resistance," and that is effectively what passive, inactive people are doing, even though they may not realize it at the time. They end up suffering in many different ways and they just blame it on a variety of things, none of which are the real problem.

Do you think you are more passive than active, or more active than passive? Explain.

_____

_____

_____

Jesus is our model, and He was far from passive. He actively sought and lived out the will of God and resisted any temptation or pressure to do otherwise. The descriptive words we attribute to God even reveal Him as active—He saves, He redeems, He heals, He provides, He helps.

Read about Mary and Martha in Luke 10:38-42. Which woman are you more like—Martha, who was hyperactive and appeared to value work more, or Mary, who knew how to lay her work aside and spend time with Jesus? Explain.

_____

_____

_____

What can you learn from both of their approaches to life?

_____

_____

We need to live well-balanced lives, and that comes from taking an active role in your spiritual life as well as your natural life.

As we spend time with God in fellowship, prayer, and Bible study, we will learn how to live properly. It helps us grow spiritually, and that is very important. Many Christians haven't made any spiritual progress since they were saved. They have a long list of bad habits they intend to give up, but they are not actively doing anything that will help them do so. Don't sit idly by and allow life to happen to you. Choose to live life "on purpose."

Go!

How much spiritual progress do you think you've made since you began your Christian journey?

_____

_____

What do you think has been helpful to your progress, and what do you think has hindered your progress?

_____

_____

_____

List several things you can do now to become more actively engaged in growing spiritually.

_____

_____

_____

How might these things help you be more engaged in your purpose?

_____

_____

_____

_____

Read the parable of the ten virgins in Matthew 25:1–12 from several versions of the Bible. Which group do you identify with most—the five wise or the five foolish virgins? Explain.

_____

_____

_____

Which church do you identify with most among the ones listed on pages 152–153 and in Revelation? Explain.

_____

_____

_____

What can you do to keep moving in the right direction and not drift in the wrong direction?

_____

_____

_____

It certainly sounds to me like if we don't keep moving in the right direction, we will drift in the wrong direction. For example, I find for myself that if I don't study scriptures on the power of words occasionally, I will once again start saying things that are destructive. If I study walking in love, I am more inclined to do it. If I study giving, I become more generous. These are all things I am fully aware of, but if I don't keep growing in God's Word, I will go backward. Christianity is about an active relationship with Christ. Church was never meant to be a spectator sport; we can all be active in the journey of life! We each have a home run waiting for us, but we have to keep swinging the bat.

Write a commitment statement to help stir yourself up, resist passivity and lethargy, and actively pursue God's will for your life.

_____

_____

_____

Remember

Passivity will keep you from enjoying the best life God has for you. In order to walk in God's plan for your life, it is important to take action steps.

For the light makes everything visible. This is why it is said,

"Awake, O sleeper, rise up from the dead, and Christ will give you light."

Ephesians 5:14 (NLT)

Be Careful How You Live

Before you begin, read chapter 16 in *Seize the Day*.

Get Ready...

Have you become more active rather than passive in pursuing your purpose since completing the previous chapter? Explain. What do you need to do to be more active?

_____

_____

_____

Read the opening verse, Ephesians 5:15, from several versions. Which group are you living like—the unwise or the wise? Explain.

_____

_____

_____

Answer the questions I suggest at the beginning of the chapter to determine how carefully you live. Remember, these questions are offered to get you thinking.

What is your lifestyle, and would Jesus approve of it?

_____

_____

_____

What are your habits, good and bad?

_____

_____

_____

Do you have a purpose? Share it.

_____

_____

_____

Are you living your life "on purpose" each day?

_____

_____

_____

Do you have a plan? Share it.

_____

_____

_____

Are you able to follow through with your plans?

_____

_____

_____

How often do you fail to accomplish your daily goals?

_____

_____

Are you leaving a legacy?

_____

_____

_____

What are you accomplishing in life?

_____

_____

_____

Get Set…

To be careful really means to be wise, to choose to do now what you will be happy with later. The Greek word that we now translate as "be careful" was originally translated "walk circumspectly." That word means to look all around, like one who is walking in a very dangerous place. This person, as he walks, is constantly observing where he should put his feet next. Each decision we make represents a step that we take in our walk with God, and we should make them very carefully, considering what the outcome may be.

Be an investor in life, not a gambler! Make right choices and be assured of eventually getting a right result—don't make wrong choices and gamble that you might get by with it. Most people who have a serious gambling habit may gamble and occasionally win, but in the end most of them lose everything.

Which areas of your life do you sense you need to make a change in?

_____

_____

_____

_____

How will you make that change?

_____

_____

Are you building a life you want your children to inherit? Are you leaving a legacy to the world you can be proud of? Explain.

_____

_____

As we choose a lifestyle, we should realize that our children more than likely will imitate what they see us do in many ways. We need to be careful how we build, not only for ourselves, but also for those we influence. Don't build your life with one of the more inferior materials, don't even choose the middle-of-the-road materials, but instead choose and prize what is excellent and of real value.

Read Ephesians 2:10 from several versions of the Bible. How do you think we are called to walk in the good life God has prearranged for us?

_____

_____

_____

Since before the beginning of what we know as "time," God has prepared or planned ahead for us to have a good life. The prerequisite to the good life is to be born again by receiving Jesus as our personal Savior through our faith. After that, God desires that we go on to live the life He has made ready for us to live. He has laid out good works that "we may do them," and He has prepared paths that "we should walk in them."

We can clearly see that the will of God is for us to do good things and live a good life. That is impossible without us having a new nature, so He gives us His very own nature through the new birth, and then says to us, "Now you choose this good plan and the good works and walk them out in your life for My glory." The message could not be any clearer: God provides, and we choose!

Go!

List five tangible ways you will choose to walk in the good life God has planned for you. Your list may include action steps you've written already; repeating them will remind you of your commitment.

_____

_____

_____

Have you been trying to be strong in faith through someone else's faith? How can you commit to building your own faith in God?

_____

_____

As I started a journey to study God's Word myself and seek God for myself, I discovered that without faith it is impossible to please God, and that everything we do should be done in faith. We may have very strong faith and still experience trials and difficulty in life. God gives us faith to get through hardship victoriously. We are more than conquerors through Christ Who loves us (see Romans 8:37), but how can we be more than conquerors if we never have anything to conquer? Faith does not eliminate difficulty, but it does help us navigate it while trusting God to deliver us at the right time.

How are you preparing for Christ's return? How does your purpose relate to your preparation?

_____

_____

_____

Read the statistics I list from George Barna and David Barton on page 164. Which ones do you think are acceptable according to God's Word? Use a concordance or online search tool to find out exactly what the Word of God says about these things.

_____

_____

_____

How can you shine your light more brightly in this world?

_____

_____

_____

How can you resist the following?…

Listening to unsound doctrine

_____

_____

Gossip

_____

_____

Associating closely with people who are bad influences

_____

_____

We do choose our friends, and it's important that we choose them wisely. Choose friends you can trust, you can admire and respect, and you would like to learn from. If we spend a lot of time with someone, we may adopt the mannerisms and habits of that person and not even be aware that we are doing it. People influence us, so it is essential that we guard our heart, for out of it flow the springs of life.

Remember

To be "careful" really means to be wise—to choose to do now what you will be happy with later.

Christians are not perfect in their behavior. We do make mistakes, but we can still strive to do our best and always remember that we are God's representatives in the earth. Let's live more carefully, being watchful and cautious, and as we do, it will not only improve our own lives, but it will also be a good example to others.

As a prisoner for the Lord, then, I urge you to live a life worthy of the calling you have received.

Ephesians 4:1 (NIV)

What Are You Doing with What God Has Given You?

Before you begin, read chapter 17 in *Seize the Day*.

Get Ready...

After completing the previous chapter, have you been more careful about how you live out the life Jesus has prepared for you? Explain.

_____

_____

_____

Read the opening quote by A. W. Tozer. Do you agree with it? Share your thoughts on wasting ourselves—what is most like God?

_____

_____

_____

Do you feel in danger of wasting your life? If so, how can you change today? If not, why not?

_____

_____

_____

Review your past week. Which days would you say you spent wasting your life? Which days would you say you spent investing in your life? Explain what you did on each day.

Monday

_____

Tuesday

_____

Wednesday

_____

Thursday

_____

Friday

_____

Saturday

_____

Sunday

_____

We are always spending something, and when we do, we are either wasting it or investing it. God doesn't want you to waste your life—He wants you to invest it and bear good fruit.

Get Set...

Read I Corinthians 1:27–29 from several versions of the Bible. Fill in the blanks according to the words found in the NIV.

But _____ chose the foolish things of the world to shame the _____; God chose the _____ things of the world to shame the strong. God chose the lowly things of this world and the _____ things—and the things that are not—to _____ the things that are, so that no one may _____ before him.

How does this verse make you feel about your adequacies and inadequacies?

_____

_____

_____

How do you rely on God's strength to live wisely?

_____

_____

_____

Perhaps you feel you don't have much, but let's remember the very small lunch that the boy offered to Jesus. Jesus multiplied it and fed thousands of people. Instead of being so concerned about what you don't have, offer to Jesus what you do have and watch Him multiply it. If we think too little of what we have, we are likely to waste it, so remember that whatever you have, it is important! You are important!

Think about what you are doing with the dash between your birthdate and death date. Write your birth year on the left side of the paper and fill in the line with what you want to do with your dash.

Birthdate   _____?   (death date)

How can you make sure your dash is filled with good choices that produce excellent results?

_____

_____

_____

Read Esther's story in Esther chapters 2–7.

   Why was she afraid to make a request to the king?

_____

_____

What changed her mind?

_____

_____

What was the outcome?

_____

_____

What characteristics of Esther do you need to imitate?

_____

_____

When we seize the opportunities that are in front of us, we realize God's reward that is attached to our obedience.

Whether the opportunities are small or large, when we are given chances to serve God, it is an honor. There are billions of people on the earth, and God can choose whomever He wants to. If He chooses you for anything, redeem the time and, as the apostle Paul said, "buy up each opportunity" (see Colossians 4:5, AMPC). We can buy an opportunity with time.

We can spend our time and use it to invest in God's plan and then reap His reward.

How often do you seize the opportunity to:

Study God's Word?

_____

Encourage someone or witness about the love of God?

_____

> Behave yourselves wisely [living prudently and with discretion] in your relations with those of the outside world (the non-Christians), making the very most of the time and seizing (buying up) the opportunity.
>
> Colossians 4:5 (AMPC)

Showing patience, kindness, and love to those we encounter daily is a very important ministry, and one we don't want to take lightly. I think each person we meet is an opportunity of some kind. Even if we merely exchange a smile, it may leave a lasting impression.

Go!

How often are you willing to slow down and share a story—or thought or word—with someone who may need encouragement? How do you make yourself attentive to the prompting of the Spirit for these opportunities?

_____

_____

_____

Being a blessing to people always takes a little time, so be sure you redeem your time and buy up each opportunity that comes your way.

How much of your money do you give?

_____

How much of your money do you spend?

_____

How much of your money do you save?

_____

What plan can you develop and implement to be able to give more? To save more?

_____

_____

We can all learn to waste less and have more respect for what God has given us. One of the ways I am trying to do that is to be sure I use what I spend money on, and if I am not going to use it, then I give it away. I also practice thinking about purchases, especially larger ones, before taking action. For some reason, a lot of things that seem so attractive in the store don't look as good when we get them home. Emotional purchases very often end up being regretted later.

What do you need to do to have more energy? Or to maximize the energy you have?

_____

_____

What are your gifts? How do you use them to benefit God and others?

_____

_____

Don't waste your life by wasting your abilities. Find employment that uses your gifts and you will love your job. We are all fulfilled and satisfied when we are doing what God intended us to do. I work hard, but I am doing what I am intended to do, and therefore, it is not stressful. It is a joy and I find fulfillment in doing it.

We are stewards of all that God gives to us, and He asks us to be faithful. He always rewards us for a job well done! More than ever, be determined not to waste your resources. Pray and ask God to show you areas where you might use more prudence. I believe that God gives us more than enough of everything we need in life, and if we manage it well, we will not lack any good thing.

Remember

What you do today is important because you are exchanging a day of your life for it.

Give, and you will receive. Your gift will return to you in full—pressed down, shaken together to make room for more, running over, and poured into your lap. The amount you give will determine the amount you get back.

Luke 6:38 (NLT)

Seeing the End from the Beginning

Before you begin, read chapter 18 in *Seize the Day*.

Get Ready...

How have you used your money, energy, and talents differently since completing the previous chapter? What would you still like to do differently?

_____

_____

_____

Read the opening quote about a successful person. Do you agree with the quote? Explain.

_____

_____

_____

On a scale of 1 to 5, rate how focused you think you are (1 is not focused at all; 5 is extremely focused).

1   2   3   4   5

Write down ideas on how you can be more focused, if need be.

_____

_____

_____

Get Set...

Read the story about Florence Chadwick that I tell on pages 181–182. How do you think she felt knowing she had stopped just one mile away from her goal?

_____

_____

_____

How did she successfully complete her goal the next time?

_____

_____

_____

What lessons from Florence's story can help you as you try to attain goals?

_____

_____

_____

Look up Proverbs 4:25 in several Bible translations. Write the one you understand the clearest. Consider posting it in a place where you will see it often, or commit it to memory.

_____

_____

_____

Focus is directed attention. It is having a goal, aiming for a target, and not being easily distracted. Focus is the determination to stay on target and not allow other things to distract you.

What are some strategies you use, or need to use, to stay more focused?

_____

_____

_____

Match the verses with the statements on the left. Which verses can help you stay focused? Write them down and commit them to memory.

God can strengthen you to have patience and endurance to complete your tasks.	Romans 12:12
Be brave and courageous as you patiently wait on God.	Philippians 3:12–14
Forget the past and keep pressing on.	Colossians 1:11
Be hopeful and pray while you wait on God to deliver you from trouble.	Psalm 27:14

Some of our spiritual goals are never completely reached in this lifetime, but we still patiently press toward them. I would love to never do anything wrong, and to love everyone perfectly, but I have not arrived and won't until I get to Heaven. But I am constrained by my love for God to keep pressing toward the goal.

Go!

How do you feel about giving up? Is it an option for you? Explain.

_____

_____

_____

I have often said the one thing I have done that has been the most helpful for me in reaching my goals is that I have not given up. It takes no special talent to give up, but it does take focus and determination to refuse to give up. Not giving up is especially difficult in the foundation-laying phase. Strong foundations are vital to the success of the remainder of what we hope to build in life.

When we plant a seed in the ground, we have given up our seed and see nothing for a long time that indicates that our sacrifice was worth it. But eventually something comes out of the ground, and it grows into a thing of beauty and amazement. It grows into something that many others can enjoy.

Draw a picture of your favorite flower. Research how long it takes for it to grow into a pretty flower. You may want to plant a seed and watch it grow to remind you to be patient and never give up.

I have had a great many goals in my life. The idea of actually reaching most of them seemed quite impossible at the outset, but many of them are a reality in my life now. I am quite ordinary, but I "keep on keeping on" and have no plans to quit. Don't let being ordinary stop or hinder you from trying to do something great. Remember that most of the men and women we read about in the Bible, those we call heroes of faith, were very ordinary. They were fishermen, tax collectors, ex-prostitutes, shepherds, maidens, and even a woman who had been demon-possessed! No one is exempt from being used by God. All it takes to succeed is faith in God and determination!

Find the story of a hero of faith in the Bible (several are listed in Hebrews 11). Read about how your hero was used by God, even though he or she was ordinary. How did your hero keep going? How can you use his or her example to remind you to keep pressing and focusing on your goals?

_____

_____

_____

_____

What are some things you will do—and some things you will not do—to focus on reaching your goals? (I hope "never give up" is included in your "do" column!)

Things I will do:

_____

_____

_____

Things I won't do:

_____

_____

_____

Remember

In order to seize the day, make goals and go after them with all your heart. Ordinary people can do extraordinary things if they apply the proper guidelines to their lives.

You can recover from mistakes because God is forgiving and merciful, but you cannot recover if you quit. Believe me when I say that we all make mistakes, and plenty of them. God knew that we would mess up, and that is precisely why He sent Jesus to forgive us and the Holy Spirit to help us.

> Don't you realize that in a race everyone runs, but only one person gets the prize? So run to win!
>
> I Corinthians 9:24 (NLT)

Finding Strength for the Journey

Before you begin, read chapter 19 in *Seize the Day.*

Get Ready...

What have you done since reading the previous chapter to become more focused on reaching your goals and seizing each day?

_____

_____

_____

Read the opening scripture, Psalm 46:1, from several translations in the Bible. What does this verse say about finding strength? In whom do we find strength?

_____

_____

_____

Do you find you have a desire to seize the day but perhaps no or little strength? Explain.

_____

_____

_____

How often do you pray specifically for God's strength to help you accomplish a goal?

_____

_____

_____

Get Set...

*Many find that they have the desire to do a thing, but no strength for the journey. God is our strength, so if we are trying to make the journey without putting Him first, we will fail. Our own strength will fail. Even youths and strong men have their limits, but with God we are unlimited as long as we stay focused on His goals for us instead of our own. We cannot do anything **we want** to do, but we can do anything **He wants** us to do!*

Read Isaiah 40:30–31 from several translations of the Bible. Then answer the questions.

What does the passage say about youth?

_____

_____

_____

Who can renew their strength?

_____

_____

_____

Describe how those who have their strength renewed will act.

_____

_____

What do you need God's power to complete?

_____

_____

_____

Read about the thorn in Paul's flesh in II Corinthians 12:7–9. What was God's answer when Paul prayed to have the thorn removed?

_____

_____

_____

How do you think God gave him grace that was sufficient to bear the trouble? (Consider what you know of Paul.)

_____

_____

_____

Write a prayer to God asking specifically for what you need.

_____

_____

_____

_____

Go!

When you ask in Jesus' name and according to His will, it will be done. Read each scripture reference and match it to its theme. Then write how these verses will help you seek the strength you need.

You have not because you ask not.	John 15:7
If you live in Christ, ask what you will and you will receive it.	John 16:24
Ask in Jesus' name and you will have joy.	John 14:13–14
If you ask, you will receive.	James 4:2

_____

_____

_____

What methods do you currently use to study the Bible? How often do you use them? How can you make more time to study God's Word for yourself? Write out a plan.

_____

_____

_____

You can enhance your church experience tenfold by making notes of the scripture verses your pastor or Bible teacher uses when sharing God's Word and then going home and looking them up and reading and meditating on them for yourself. In addition to studying God's Word personally, also surround yourself with good resources that contain the Word of God taught by someone who is anointed by God to teach. Devotionals, books, and recorded messages are good resources. Even plaques displayed in your home that have scripture verses on them are beneficial.

Do you believe the quote by Charles Buxton: *You will never find time for anything. If you want time, you must make it?* How will you *make* time for Bible study and intentional time with God?

_____

_____

_____

Remember

In order to bear good fruit in any area of life, just stay connected to the Vine (Jesus).

The best thing you can do to make the most of each day is to start that day with God.

> [Paul said,] "God did this so that they would seek him and perhaps reach out for him and find him, though he is not far from any one of us. 'For in him we live and move and have our being.' As some of your own poets have said, 'We are his offspring.'"
>
> Acts 17:27–28 (NIV)

Seize Your Thoughts

Before you begin, read chapter 20 in *Seize the Day.*

Get Ready…

Have you found renewed strength since completing the previous chapter to seize the day and accomplish your goals? Explain.

_____

_____

_____

Read the opening verse, II Corinthians 10:5, in several versions. What do we want our thoughts to be in line with? Why is this important?

_____

_____

_____

Why do you think it is so important for us to take control of our thoughts?

_____

_____

_____

How often do you bring your thoughts in line with what is obedient to Christ? What times—or during what circumstances—do you need particular help to bring your thoughts in line with Christ?

_____

_____

_____

Get Set...

What does it mean that the weapons of warfare are not physical? (See II Corinthians 10:4.)

_____

_____

_____

If the weapons are not physical, how effective will it be to deal with them physically? How should we deal with spiritual warfare?

_____

_____

_____

What spiritual weapons do you use to bring your thoughts captive and in line with Christ?

_____

_____

_____

We have weapons that will destroy strongholds when used properly. Using these weapons, we are to cast down all wrong thoughts. Our weapon is the Word of God, and it can be used in a variety of ways. We can compare our thoughts to the Word, and when those thoughts don't agree, we make an adjustment and *come into agreement with God. We can meditate on the Word, which helps to renew our minds and think good and beneficial things. We can also confess the Word out loud and it helps us by interrupting any wrong thought pattern we are experiencing. We may also pray the Word! We can fill our prayers with scriptures, putting God in remembrance of His promises as He has instructed us to do. We may also hear the Word of God or read it, and it will keep our minds renewed to God's plan for our lives.*

The Word of God is referred to as "the Sword of the Spirit" in the Bible. Swords are used in battle, and they should always be sharp and close at hand for use. I urge you to remember that God's Word is a weapon for you to use against Satan.

Read Ephesians 6:10–18 from several versions of the Bible. List the equipment described in the armor of God.

_____

_____

_____

_____

How can you equip yourself with each piece of the armor?

_____

_____

_____

Go!

You can do your own thinking. You can choose your own thoughts and should do so carefully. You can choose to think about a thing or not to think about it. All thoughts are seeds that we sow, and they will bring a harvest in our life. All seed bears fruit after its own kind, so don't sow what you don't want a crop of.

If we sow a tomato seed, we expect to get a tomato, but if we sow thoughts of hatred and anger, we often expect to have a great and joyful life. That will never happen! Sowing thoughts of anger and hatred will produce a bitter, miserable life. The world is filled with people who have miserable lives, but they often merely blame their circumstances on others instead of searching their own heart to discover what the true roots of their problems are.

Draw a picture of what you want to sow to remind you to plant thoughts in line with the kind of harvest you want to reap.

Read Romans 12:2, NIV. Fill in the missing words.

Do not _____ to the pattern of this world, but be _____ by the renewing of your _____. Then you will be able to test and _____ what God's _____ is—his good, pleasing and _____ will.

How do you renew your mind?

_____

_____

_____

How do your words help you keep your mind renewed and in line with God's will?

_____

_____

_____

Review the ten power thoughts I have listed on pages 206–207. Write the ones that will help you the most to remember and repeat each day. You may also add a few of your own.

_____

_____

_____

_____

Remember

We cannot seize the day unless we are willing to seize and take captive any thought that is contrary to God's Word.

The more you practice right thinking, the more natural it becomes.

May these words of my mouth and this meditation of my heart be pleasing in your sight, Lord, my Rock and my Redeemer.

Psalm 19:14 (NIV)

Five Things to Do on Purpose

Before you begin, read chapter 21 in *Seize the Day*.

Get Ready…

Have you been more intentional about your words and thoughts since completing the previous chapter? Explain.

_____

_____

_____

Read the opening verse, Ephesians 6:13, from several translations. How has identifying and putting on parts of the armor of God helped you seize the day and your thoughts?

_____

_____

_____

Do you believe you have to be active rather than passive in the fight to live the good life? Explain.

_____

_____

_____

Do you think the fight is worth it? Explain.

_____

_____

_____

Get Set...

Think of a time when you had to talk yourself down from the ledge. Explain how you did it. Was it worth it?

_____

_____

_____

For many years I was deceived and thought that if my circumstances didn't calm down I couldn't calm down. By thinking in this way I was literally giving the devil control over my behavior. If he set me up to get upset by arranging for circumstances that were unpleasant for me, then I had an anxious and frustrating day. We need to know what our "peace-stealers" are and watch out for them.

What are your "peace-stealers" or trigger points that may keep you from peace?

_____

_____

_____

How can you prepare to deal with these triggers before they occur?

_____

_____

_____

Read the following passages. Write how remembering each one can help with your peace-stealing triggers.

John 14:27

_____

_____

I Peter 5:9

_____

_____

James 1:19

_____

_____

When you are tempted to sin—or actually do—how do you remember who you are in Christ, seek forgiveness, and move on?

_____

_____

We see the phrase "put on" several times in the Bible and I have come to understand that it simply means "Do this on purpose." Don't wait to feel like it or expect someone else to do for us what we should do ourselves. Rather than being passive, seize or take control of the situation, your thoughts and attitudes, and line them up with God's promises.

You are a beloved child of God, the apple of His eye, and He is with you at all times. Don't let the devil steal your true identity. Know who you are, hold your head up confidently, and enjoy the life that Jesus has provided for you. Do it on purpose!

Read Colossians 3:12–14. What virtues should we strive to put on? Why do you think love is the most important virtue?

_____

_____

_____

_____

The most important thing we can do is to walk in love. Love is not a feeling we wait to have, it is a decision we make about how we will treat people—all people! We don't get to treat people who are good to us one way and then mistreat the ones who are rude and unkind to us. Like God, we should be the same all the time no matter what is happening around us.

Yes, I know that is a tall order, but we will never do anything God asks us to do if we keep telling ourselves how hard it is to do it. We can choose to believe that God will enable us to do anything He asks us to do.

Walking in love will require being generous in forgiveness, because the truth is we live in a world filled with imperfection. People hurt us, they may treat us unjustly, or be unloving to us, but God has given us a simple solution to not allowing the poison of bitterness into our souls. Jesus told us not only to forgive our enemies, but to be kind and good to them!

Go!

How can you purpose to pray about everything? What reminders can you use to pray always?

_____

_____

_____

Read Philippians 4:6 from several versions of the Bible. Write the one below that you will commit to memory or keep in a place where you can see it often.

_____

_____

_____

Write your prayer requests at this time. As you write, pray over your concerns.

_____

_____

_____

What can you do when you grow weary of doing right and living on purpose? (See Galatians 6:9.)

_____

_____

_____

The greatest hindrance to spiritual maturity is walking according to our emotions instead of purposely choosing to do the right thing. Even though we may not want to do a thing, we can choose to do it just because we love God.

Remember

The most important thing you can do is to walk in love.
  You can meet any crisis with the faith that is released in prayer.

Rejoice always, pray continually, give thanks in all circumstances; for this is God's will for you in Christ Jesus.

I Thessalonians 5:16–18 (NIV)

Take Charge of Your Life

Before you begin, read chapter 22 in *Seize the Day*.

Get Ready...

Now that you have read the entire book and completed this study guide, how has your life changed? What things are you doing to seize the day? What impact have they had on your life?

_____

_____

_____

_____

Read the opening quote. How are you bridging the gap between who you are and who you want to be?

_____

_____

_____

Take some time and ask yourself the questions I ask on page 221.

    What am I living for?

_____

_____

_____

Who am I living for?

_____

_____

_____

Am I prepared to meet God?

_____

_____

_____

When I die, will I leave a legacy to be proud of?

_____

_____

_____

Am I enjoying my life?

_____

_____

_____

If you don't get the answers you want, then you need to take charge of your life and start living "on purpose" for a purpose!

Get Set...

Read Matthew 7:13–14. Have you chosen the narrow road? What are some differences between traveling the narrow road and the wide road?

_____

_____

_____

Ask yourself the questions I asked my staff:

What do you need to take charge of in your life?

_____

_____

_____

What are the things/circumstances that keep you from taking control of those areas?

_____

_____

_____

What actions will you take today to make the needed changes?

_____

_____

_____

Putting off taking action until tomorrow, or at another time in life, is not wise. The sooner you make a change, the sooner you will be living the life you truly want to live.

The discipline of making the right choice no matter how one feels is the road to a successful life. Seizing the day is all about making the best choices possible each day of your life. What you have today is a result of choices made in the past, and what you have in the future will be the result of choices you make now!

How can asking yourself about the end before you begin help you make the best decision? (For example, thinking about the end result before you begin?)

_____

_____

_____

Go!

When we make good choices, they may not always appear to be good immediately. We often have to add patience into the mix and trust God that right choices always produce a right result if we won't give up. Doing something right once or twice never brings the result we desire. We must be committed to a lifestyle of making right choices over and above all else. This is living on the narrow path that will lead to the life we desire.

Discipline doesn't seem joyful immediately, but it will produce the peace of right living in due time.

Read Hebrews 12:11, NLT. Fill in the missing words. Then journal your thoughts about discipline.

No _____ is enjoyable while it is _____ it's painful! But _____ there will be a _____ harvest of right living for those who are _____ in this way.

_____

_____

_____

It feels really good to know that you are using your time wisely and accomplishing something worthwhile in life. It feels good to make wise decisions rather than living riotously and then feeling condemned because of it. No matter how people may choose to avoid the reality of it, the bottom line is that we feel good when we are doing what we know we should be doing and we feel bad when we don't. The world is filled with people who make wrong decisions and then, when they don't like the result of the choices they have made, they find a way to blame their unfulfilled life on someone or something else. They may medicate or numb their dissatisfaction in some way, but it will always return again and again to renew their misery.

However, even if you feel that you have wasted a lot of your life, all is not lost! Anyone can make a choice and change the direction he or she has been taking in life. We can all start today making right choices in line with God's will for our life. Every good and right decision that we make helps overturn the results of the bad ones. God's will always produces good results, so you can get started immediately turning your life around for the better.

What boundaries do you have in place in the following areas of your life?

Eating

_____

_____

Health

_____

_____

Finances

_____

_____

Relationships (spouse, family, friends, children)

_____

_____

_____

If we have no boundaries we always become excessive in one direction or another.

Spend time with God and come up with a plan of what you desire to accomplish in life and set boundaries that will help you accomplish it.

Journal your thoughts on my final words in *Seize the Day*. How will you live life today?

Nothing good happens by accident!

Good things occur as we make choices that promote good results. Living life on purpose is actually very exciting! It gives us a feeling of being a disciplined person, and we all like that feeling. When we make good decisions, it gives us the joy of partnering with God in having the best life we possibly can have. Take charge of your life under the leadership of the Holy Spirit and start enjoying every day of your new powerful, focused, and fruitful life.

_____

_____

_____

_____

_____

_____

Remember

We can spend our lives wishing, but wishing won't change anything. You have to take charge of your life.

That's the whole story. Here now is my final conclusion:

Fear God and obey his commands, for this is everyone's duty.

Ecclesiastes 12:13 (NLT)

Live your life "on purpose" for a purpose, and with God's help, use the free will God has given you to choose His will! As you do so, it will honor Him greatly, and you will enjoy a satisfying reward!

Do you have a real relationship with Jesus?

God loves you! He created you to be a special, unique, one-of-a-kind individual, and He has a specific purpose and plan for your life. And through a personal relationship with your Creator—God—you can discover a way of life that will truly satisfy your soul.

No matter who you are, what you've done, or where you are in your life right now, God's love and grace are greater than your sin—your mistakes. Jesus willingly gave His life so you can receive forgiveness from God and have new life in Him. He's just waiting for you to invite Him to be your Savior and Lord.

If you are ready to commit your life to Jesus and follow Him, all you have to do is ask Him to forgive your sins and give you a fresh start in the life you are meant to live. Begin by praying this prayer...

Lord Jesus, thank You for giving Your life for me and forgiving me of my sins so I can have a personal relationship with You. I am sincerely sorry for the mistakes I've made, and I know I need You to help me live right.

Your Word says in Romans 10:9, "If you declare with your mouth, 'Jesus is Lord,' and believe in your heart that God raised him from the dead, you will be saved" (NIV). I believe You are the Son of God and confess You as my Savior and Lord. Take me just as I am, and work in my heart, making me the person You want me to be. I want to live for You, Jesus, and I am so grateful that You are giving me a fresh start in my new life with You today.

I love You, Jesus!

It's so amazing to know that God loves us so much! He wants to have a deep, intimate relationship with us that grows every day as we spend time with Him in prayer and Bible study. And we want to encourage you in your new life in Christ.

Please visit joycemeyer.org/salvation to request Joyce's book *A New Way of Living*, which is our gift to you. We also have other free resources online to help you make progress in pursuing everything God has for you.

Congratulations on your fresh start in your life in Christ! We hope to hear from you soon.

JOYCE MEYER is one of the world's leading practical Bible teachers. Her daily broadcast, *Enjoying Everyday Life*, airs on hundreds of television networks and radio stations worldwide.

Joyce has written more than one hundred inspirational books. Her best-sellers include *Power Thoughts*; *The Confident Woman*; *Look Great, Feel Great*; *Starting Your Day Right*; *Ending Your Day Right*; *Approval Addiction*; *How to Hear from God*; *Beauty for Ashes*; and *Battlefield of the Mind*.

Joyce travels extensively, holding conferences throughout the year and speaking to thousands around the world.

Joyce Meyer Ministries
P.O. Box 655
Fenton, MO 63026
USA
(636) 349-0303

Joyce Meyer Ministries—Canada
P.O. Box 7700
Vancouver, BC V6B 4E2
Canada
(800) 868-1002

Joyce Meyer Ministries—Australia
Locked Bag 77
Mansfield Delivery Centre
Queensland 4122
Australia
(07) 3349 1200

Joyce Meyer Ministries—England
P.O. Box 1549
Windsor SL4 1GT
United Kingdom
01753 831102

Joyce Meyer Ministries—South Africa
P.O. Box 5
Cape Town 8000
South Africa
(27) 21-701-1056

100 Ways to Simplify Your Life
21 Ways to Finding Peace and Happiness
Any Minute
Approval Addiction
The Approval Fix
The Battle Belongs to the Lord
*Battlefield of the Mind**
Battlefield of the Mind for Kids
Battlefield of the Mind for Teens
Battlefield of the Mind Devotional
*Be Anxious for Nothing**
Being the Person God Made You to Be
Beauty for Ashes
Change Your Words, Change Your Life
The Confident Mom
The Confident Woman
The Confident Woman Devotional
Do Yourself a Favor . . . Forgive
Eat the Cookie . . . Buy the Shoes
Eight Ways to Keep the Devil Under Your Feet
Ending Your Day Right
Enjoying Where You Are on the Way to Where You Are Going
The Everyday Life Bible
Filled with the Spirit
Get Your Hopes Up!
Good Health, Good Life
Hearing from God Each Morning
*How to Hear from God**
How to Succeed at Being Yourself
I Dare You
*If Not for the Grace of God**
In Pursuit of Peace
The Joy of Believing Prayer
Knowing God Intimately
A Leader in the Making
Life in the Word
Living Beyond Your Feelings
Living Courageously
Look Great, Feel Great
Love Out Loud
The Love Revolution
Making Good Habits, Breaking Bad Habits
Making Marriage Work (previously published as *Help Me—I'm Married!*)
*Me and My Big Mouth!**
*The Mind Connection**
Never Give Up!
Never Lose Heart
New Day, New You
*Overload**

The Penny
Perfect Love (previously published as *God Is Not Mad at You*)*
The Power of Being Positive
The Power of Being Thankful
The Power of Determination
The Power of Forgiveness
The Power of Simple Prayer
Power Thoughts
Power Thoughts Devotional
Power Words
Reduce Me to Love
The Secret Power of Speaking God's Word
The Secrets of Spiritual Power
The Secret to True Happiness
Seven Things That Steal Your Joy
Start Your New Life Today
Starting Your Day Right
Straight Talk
Teenagers Are People Too!
Trusting God Day by Day
The Word, the Name, the Blood
Woman to Woman
You Can Begin Again

JOYCE MEYER SPANISH TITLES

Belleza en Lugar de Cenizas (*Beauty for Ashes*)
Buena Salud, Buena Vida (*Good Health, Good Life*)
Cambia Tus Palabras, Cambia Tu Vida (*Change Your Words, Change Your Life*)
El Campo de Batalla de la Mente (*Battlefield of the Mind*)
Como Formar Buenos Habitos y Romper Malos Habitos
(*Making Good Habits, Breaking Bad Habits*)
La Conexión de la Mente (*The Mind Connection*)
Dios No Está Enojado Contigo (*God Is Not Mad at You*)
La Dosis de Aprobación (*The Approval Fix*)
Empezando Tu Día Bien (*Starting Your Day Right*)
Hazte Un Favor a Ti Mismo…Perdona (*Do Yourself a Favor…Forgive*)
Madre Segura de sí Misma (*The Confident Mom*)
Palabras de Poder (*Power Words*)
Pensamientos de Poder (*Power Thoughts*)
Sobrecarga (*Overload*)
Termina Bien Tu Día (*Ending Your Day Right*)
Usted Puede Comenzar de Nuevo (*You Can Begin Again*)
¡Viva con Esperanza! (*Get Your Hopes Up!*)
Viva Valientemente (*Living Courageously*)

*Study Guide available for this title

BOOKS BY DAVE MEYER

Life Lines